June 16, 1992

Janet and Greg,

Perhaps you can find
an interesting place to stay
after you meet in Alabama.

Enjoy!    Love,
          Shirley/Mother
                    and
          Paul

# HISTORIC INNS *of the* SOUTH

**CRESCENT BOOKS**
New York

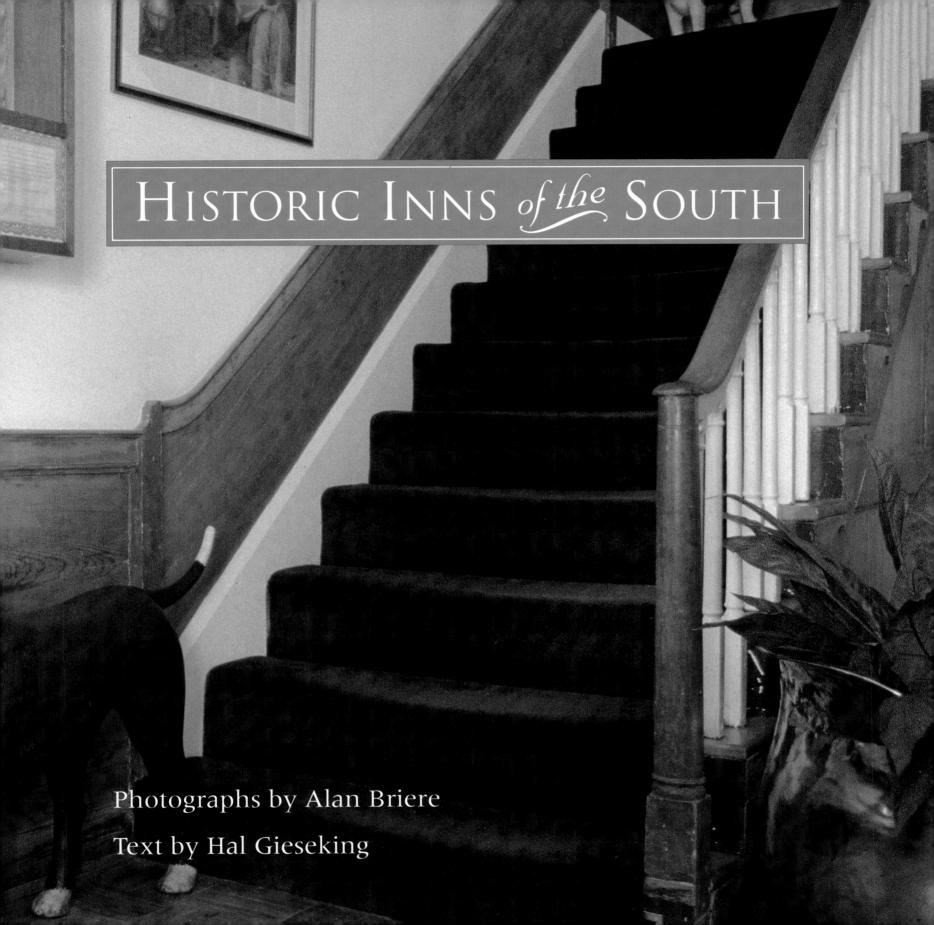

# HISTORIC INNS *of the* SOUTH

Photographs by Alan Briere

Text by Hal Gieseking

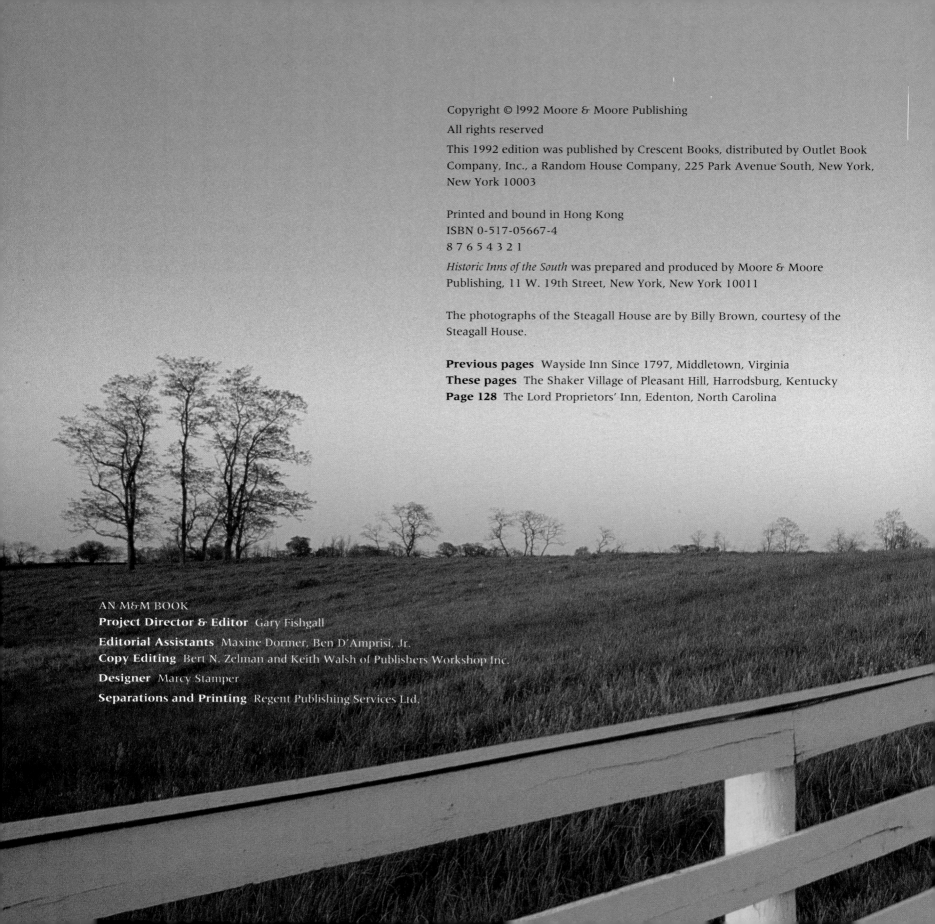

This 1992 edition was published by Crescent Books, distributed by Outlet Book Company, Inc., a Random House Company, 225 Park Avenue South, New York, New York 10003

Printed and bound in Hong Kong
ISBN 0-517-05667-4
8 7 6 5 4 3 2 1

*Historic Inns of the South* was prepared and produced by Moore & Moore Publishing, 11 W. 19th Street, New York, New York 10011

The photographs of the Steagall House are by Billy Brown, courtesy of the Steagall House.

**Previous pages**  Wayside Inn Since 1797, Middletown, Virginia
**These pages**  The Shaker Village of Pleasant Hill, Harrodsburg, Kentucky
**Page 128**  The Lord Proprietors' Inn, Edenton, North Carolina

AN M&M BOOK
**Project Director & Editor**  Gary Fishgall
**Editorial Assistants**  Maxine Dormer, Ben D'Amprisi, Jr.
**Copy Editing**  Bert N. Zelman and Keith Walsh of Publishers Workshop Inc.
**Designer**  Marcy Stamper
**Separations and Printing**  Regent Publishing Services Ltd.

# Contents

# *Introduction*

THERE IS NOTHING WHICH HAS YET BEEN CONTRIVED BY MAN,<br/>
BY WHICH SO MUCH HAPPINESS IS PRODUCED AS BY A GOOD TAVERN OR INN.

Samuel Johnson, *Celebrated English writer and conversationalist*

DOWN THROUGH THE AGES, many travelers finding shelter along the road would have agreed with Dr. Johnson.

Almost from the beginning of recorded history, there have been inns. In the days of the Roman Empire, merchants and tax collectors rested at early versions of the inn called *mansiones*. In the 13th century Marco Polo found a well-developed system of trailside inns in China. Monasteries of the Middle Ages offered cold travelers blanket space around a fire and a hot bowl from the common pot.

The English refined the art of innkeeping, introducing comfortable lodging, tables covered with roasts, breads, and vegetables, and musical entertainment. These inns spread to the new British colonies in America and later leapfrogged across the new nation along the paths of stagecoaches, canals, and eventually trains and automobiles.

Some of the American inns that welcome travelers today originated as large private homes, or gristmills, factories, and livery stables.

Many of them played major roles in American history. In the meeting rooms of some of these lodging places, early patriots gathered to plot the overthrow of British rule. Some inns of the South literally became part of the Civil War, as centers of political unrest, and then as headquarters, officers clubs, and hospitals for Confederate or Union armies.

This book will introduce you to many of the most historic inns of the South, all still welcoming travelers.

The oldest site that we will visit is the Casa de Solana in St. Augustine, Florida, built in 1763 by a direct descendant of the first colonial child born in America. The youngest is the Boar's Head Inn & Sports Club in Charlottesville, Virginia, built in 1963. But even this relative newcomer has historic roots. Its dining room was once a gristmill that the Union army tried, unsuccessfully, to burn to the ground in the 1860s. It was saved by a rainstorm.

Many of the inns are woven into the warp and woof of American life. Their construction dates become even more meaningful when related to current events happening around them. In 1859, for example, when workers were hoisting beams for the Nottoway Plantation in Mississippi, abolitionist John Brown and his followers were seizing an arsenal in Harpers Ferry, Virginia (now West Virginia).

In 1896, when the York House was being built in Georgia, a "movie" was being projected on a public screen for the first time in America, in New York City.

These historic inns are "snapshots" of their era, mortar-frame and brick museums of Colonial, Federal, Empire, Victorian, and Beaux-Arts styles. Unlike so many modern hotel rooms stamped from the same "cookie cutter" design, their rooms are filled with antique surprises.

This book relates stories about the many famous people and events associated with the inns. For example, Béla Bartók composed one of his concertos at the Albemarle Inn in Asheville, North Carolina. Guests pausing on the porch of the Burn in Natchez, Mississippi, may feel their spines tingle a little when they realize they are standing where Gen. Ulysses S. Grant once stood. There are even a few good ghost stories.

The photographs and text of *Historic Inns of the South* can be used and enjoyed by readers on several different levels—as an introduction to the many events in American history witnessed by these venerable lodgings, as an illustrated source of early architectural and interior design ideas, and as a practical travel guide with addresses and reservation phone numbers.

We encourage you to make these historic inns part of your personal history.

(Opposite)  *The courtyard of the Burn, Natchez, Mississippi.*

# Wayside Inn Since 1797

## MIDDLETOWN, VIRGINIA

Traveling "first class" in the late 18th century didn't offer the same perks as it does today.

Often it meant endless hours of unexpected bounces, dust, and cold drafts in a stagecoach. But at least coach travelers on the Old Black Bear Trail in Virginia rode over historic countryside, the same land surveyed by George Washington when he was a colonel in the Virginia militia. Despite the beautiful mountain scenery, passengers probably breathed easier when they finally pulled into the regular stagecoach stop, Wilkerson's Tavern. There they could look forward to a fireside dinner of spoon bread, peanut soup, and country ham, and a night in a canopied bed.

Visitors to the same hostelry (renamed the Wayside Inn Since 1797) can still enjoy all of these pleasures. The dinner is even served by waitresses in period clothing.

**BUILT IN 1797**

*The same year that Philadelphia became the first U.S. city to construct a centralized water system.*

The three-story building has guest and public rooms filled with Early American, Victorian, and Empire antiques. The four-poster beds have been carved with cannonball and acorn details. Chairs and tables may be French Provincial or Greek Revival.

One unusual feature about this inn is that guests can literally shop for antiques right from their beds. Every antique in every room is for sale.

Meals are served in seven different intimate dining rooms, with American pewter and cast-iron decorative pieces enlivening each.

The Wayside Inn Since 1797 offers the same kind of comfortable pampering once provided stagecoach travelers. But getting there now is a lot less bumpy.

*The dining room and stairway reflect the history of the Virginia countryside, traversed at various times by the likes of George Washington and Stonewall Jackson.*

(Opposite) *Stagecoaches once discharged and received passengers in front of Wilkerson's Tavern, now reborn as the Wayside Inn.*

At the Wayside, seven intimate dining rooms, including the one seen here, offer regional American cuisine.
(Opposite)  After a day of touring nearby Civil War battlefields, guests can swap "war stories" in the parlor.

(Above)  *Guests who wish to can return home with antiques that they find in their accommodations. The Wayside offers most of the guest room furnishings for purchase.*

(Right)  *Guest chambers at the Wayside offer everything from canopied four-poster beds to working fireplaces.*

*Wayside Inn Since 1797*

**7783 Main Street
Middletown, VA 22645
Reservations: 703/869-1797**

**15 guest rooms, 5 staterooms and 2 suites. All meals are available.**

# The Boar's Head Inn & Sports Club

## CHARLOTTESVILLE, VIRGINIA

In 1865 the Civil War was nearing its chaotic end in Virginia.

Gen. Ulysses S. Grant and a rising young Union officer named George Armstrong Custer wearily surveyed some manufacturing plants in the rain-drenched foothills of the Blue Ridge Mountains near Charlottesville, Virginia. Finally Grant gave the order. Burn them.

But the continuing rain saved an old 1834 mill built on the Hardware River near Thomas Jefferson's Monticello. The wet wood wouldn't burn.

More than a century later the founders of the new Boar's Head Inn had each piece of the mill numbered and taken apart. The building was then constructed on the site of the new inn.

Today the mill is the dining room and social center of an inn complex and sports club that sprawls over 54 acres with more than 190 public and guest rooms. The sports facilities include some 17 tennis courts (three indoors), four swimming pools, and basketball and squash courts—plus an adjacent golf course.

**COMPLETED IN 1963**

*The same year the New York Mets baseball team played its second and final year in the Polo Grounds. The team lost 111 of 160 games played.*

Many of the guest rooms have chestnut paneling, Colonial-style furniture, and fireplaces. The landscaped grounds are a delight, with oak, dogwood, sycamore, maple, and pine trees, accented by azalea, Virginia magnolia, and chrysanthemum—to name just a few flowering species in profusion here.

The overall image is reminiscent of an English hunt club. The symbol of the inn, the head of a boar, is a sign of hospitality that dates back to the days of Shakespeare's England.

Dinner guests today shouldn't be too bothered if it happens to rain during a meal. It was such weather that saved the lovely old pine-planked dining room some 127 years ago.

*The boar's head, a prime example of which hangs in the lounge of the Boar's Head Inn, has been a symbol of hospitality since the days of William Shakespeare.*

(Opposite) *Located in the foothills of Virginia's Blue Ridge Mountains, the Boar's Head Inn is surrounded by a rainbow of southern flowers.*

(Below) *Fireside dining is available in an historic old grist mill, one of the inn's three restaurants.*

(Right, above) *The Boar's Head's public areas are decorated with antiques purchased in England.*

(Right, below) *Pictured here is one of the inn's 175 guest chambers. Each features custom-designed furniture, created to evoke the atmosphere of a country estate.*

*The Boar's Head Inn & Sports Club*

P.O. Box 5307
Charlottesville, VA 22905
Reservations: 804/296-2181

175 guest rooms (24 with fireplaces). 3 dining rooms. All meals are available.

# The Inn at Narrow Passage

## WOODSTOCK, VIRGINIA

SOMETIMES THE VERY LOCATION of an inn will preordain a major role for it in history. Such a place is the Inn at Narrow Passage in Woodstock, Virginia.

In the 1740s early German settlers in Virginia simply wanted to build a sturdy log cabin near a convenient boat landing along the Shenandoah River.

But because of its strategic location, the building soon became an inn and a refuge for travelers fleeing Indian raiding parties that swept down from the Alleghenies. A tunnel leading toward the river was even dug in the basement to create an escape route for the occupants.

Years later the inn became a stagecoach stop, and later played an historic part in the Civil War as headquarters for "Stonewall" Jackson's Shenandoah Valley campaign of 1862.

But by 1983 all of the inn's original glory had crumbled into a decaying wreck. That was when Ed and Ellen Markel discovered the building and fell in love with its location and history.

Today the Markel's have completely restored the building, keeping the original exposed log walls, the huge limestone fireplaces, blown glass windows, and pine floors. They have added two wings and some conveniences that General Jackson might well have appreciated such as central air conditioning and heating.

The guest rooms are furnished with Early American pine reproductions, including pencil post and sleigh beds. Many of the rooms have wood-burning stoves.

The growing number of Civil War buffs who stop here may want to visit the nearby New Market Battlefield, site of an annual battle reenactment that is one of the largest in the nation.

**BUILT CIRCA 1740/41**

*The same period as that in which the first symphony orchestra in America was formed, at Bethlehem, Pennsylvania.*

*This photo offers a close-up view of the original limestone fireplace mantle in the inn's parlor.*
(Opposite) *The dining room's original pine floors and exposed ceiling beams have been restored to their 18th-century glory.*

(Above) *Gen. Thomas Jackson may once have pored over battle maps in this room, which is now the inn's parlor. The building served as Stonewall's headquarters during the Civil War Valley Campaign of 1862.*

(Left) *The inn's entrance, which now welcomes vacationers, once gave shelter to early settlers fleeing Indian war parties coming down from the Alleghenies.*

*The Inn at Narrow Passage*
**U.S. 11 South**
**Woodstock, VA 22664**
**Reservations: 703/459-8000**

12 guest rooms, 8 with private baths. A full country breakfast is included in the rates.

(Below)  *A reminder of the inn's 18th-century origins can be found in the form of a water pump in the garden.*

(Right)  *If only walls could talk. . . . These logs date back to 1740.*

# The Williamsburg Inn

## WILLIAMSBURG, VIRGINIA

IN THE MID-1930S, John D. Rockefeller, Jr., the guiding financial force behind the restoration of Colonial Williamsburg, faced a new challenge—creating an inn to serve those who were coming to see the former capital of Virginia that he had helped bring back to life.

He pondered over many architectural sketches and was particularly concerned about the bedrooms. "I shall not be happy to go forward with the Williamsburg Inn," he wrote to the architects, "until I feel that the most possible has been made of each room as regards comfort, convenience and charm."

Other strict guidelines were established. The inn had to be impressive and beautiful but should not compete with Colonial Williamsburg's important historic structures, such as the Governor's Palace and the Capitol.

The result of all this painstaking care was everything Mr. Rockefeller and thousands of visitors could desire.

**BUILT IN 1936/37**

*The same period as that in which the Democratic Party renominated Franklin D. Roosevelt for president and the American people reelected him (to his second term)*

A combination of Regency and Federal styles grace the exterior of the Williamsburg Inn, whose brick is whitewashed to separate the building in time and appearance from the nearby colonial structures. A row of stately trees at the front of the grounds form a visual barrier from the restored area.

Inside, the light wall colors and Regency furnishings create the feeling of a small European hotel. Carpets are careful reproductions of floor coverings once imported to America by the very wealthy. Fresh flower arrangements abound. No two guest rooms share the same decor.

Even Mr. Rockefeller might have been somewhat awed by a list of the inn's past guests. They include Queen Elizabeth II, Emperor Hirohito of Japan, queens from Greece and Thailand, presidents from Mexico, Italy, Paraguay, and Indonesia, and five American chief executives.

*The inn's white exterior distinguishes it visually from the unpainted 18th-century buildings in neighboring Colonial Williamsburg.*
*(Opposite) In 1946, nine years after the Colonial Williamsburg Inn opened, Reader's Digest called it "perhaps the most perfectly appointed hotel in America."*

*This parlor has welcomed an extraordinary variety of guests, ranging from Queen Elizabeth II and the emperor of Japan to five U. S. presidents.*

*A table for two beckons visitors to the dining room, which was completely remodeled recently.*

*Some of the Colonial Williamsburg Inn's corridors feature a single piece of furniture, used to accent the inn's open, airy feeling. Seen here is the area leading to the parlor.*

*This is a view of the inn's engaging courtyard as seen from a window in the parlor.*

(Below)  *This living room in one of the suites reflects the philosophy of John D. Rockefeller, Jr. who commissioned the construction of the inn. He believed that every room should represent the ultimate in "comfort convenience and charm."*

(Right)  *A statue of a woman bearing sheaves of wheat overlooks the inn's courtyard and the fairways of the golf course.*

(Pages 22 and 23)  *The Colonial Williamsburg Inn's stately lobby boasts comfortable Regency-style furnishings arranged in cozy conversational groupings.*

*The Williamsburg Inn*
**Colonial Williamsburg**
**P.O. Box B**
**Williamsburg, VA 23187**
**Reservations: 800/447-8679**

**171 guest rooms, with complete resort facilities including golf, tennis, and swimming.**

*The cooper's shop, where barrels were once made, is one of the original 19th-century buildings in the Shaker village at Pleasant Hill.*

# The Shaker Village of Pleasant Hill

## HARRODSBURG, KENTUCKY

WHERE WOULD WE BE WITHOUT THE "SHAKERS"? Possibly without wooden clothes pins, flat brooms, circular saws, or washing machines.

This famous early-American religious group invented all of these 19th-century work savers and pioneered concepts of communal ownership and racial and sexual equality.

In 1805 the Shakers started a new village at the center of 2,700 acres of Kentucky farmland about 25 miles from Lexington. By 1850 more than 30 buildings had been erected, including a 40-room Centre Family Dwelling, a white frame Meeting House, and a brick Trustees' Office. By 1910 only 12 aging members of the celibate Shakers remained, and the buildings were soon abandoned. In 1961 a nonprofit group of concerned local citizens stepped in to save the struc-

### STARTED IN 1805
*The same year that Zebulon Pike started his search for the source of the Mississippi River.*

tures as a living history museum. The U.S. Department of the Interior designated this entire complex a National Historic Landmark.

Today guests can stay in guest rooms in 15 of the original 19th-century buildings. Each of the structures and all of the reproduced Shaker furnishings in the village have the plain, simple lines that helped Shaker designs inspire so many of today's architects and furniture manufacturers.

Guests can take a walking tour of the whole area (for a fee), learn about early Shaker life, and watch demonstrations of everything from hearth cooking to tinsmithing. They also can cruise the nearby Kentucky River on the *Dixie Belle* sternwheeler that churns out from the Historic Shaker Landing, and dine on hearty Kentucky fare in the Trustees' Office, now a restaurant.

*The Shakers believed that furnishings should be finely crafted but simple and utilitarian. That philosophy is reflected in the table and staircase seen here.*

## The Shaker Village of Pleasant Hill

**3500 Lexington Road**
**Harrodsburg, KY 40330**
**Reservations: 606/734-5411**

81 guest rooms scattered among the historic buildings. Breakfast, lunch, and dinner are served at fixed-time seatings, and a children's menu is available for youngsters under 12 years of age.

(Opposite, far left) *The Centre Family Dwelling is the hub of the Shaker village, which is set on 2,700 acres of Kentucky farmland.*

(Opposite, left) *Guests at Shaker Village can stay in bedrooms once occupied by members of the sect. The one pictured here is in the East Family Dwelling.*

(Above) *Always practical, the Shakers stored their chairs on their walls when they were not in use. Historic interpreters are available throughout the village to explain and demonstrate other Shaker customs.*

# Amos Shinkle Townhouse

## COVINGTON, KENTUCKY

ALTHOUGH THEY LIVED in different centuries, Amos Shinkle and Bernie Moorman had a great deal in common.

Both were local movers and shakers.

In the mid-19th century, Amos Shinkle's company constructed an engineering masterpiece, the Roebling Suspension Bridge that stretched from Covington, Kentucky, to Cincinnati, Ohio. The bridge ended almost within cheering range of what is now Cincinnati's Riverfront Stadium, but it began on the Kentucky side just two blocks from a spacious Greco-Italianate town house constructed by Mr. Shinkle.

More than 130 years after the completion of the house, Bernie Moorman, a former mayor of Covington, began a careful restoration of the two-story structure. The ornamental cast-iron fences and gate were preserved, bordering a freshly painted bright-cream and blue-green exterior.

One of Mr. Shinkle's early decorating touches, a wall mural, still delights guests as they ascend the staircase. Each of the three guest rooms has beautiful crown molding and its own fireplace. Another four guest rooms are available in the converted carriage house behind the town house.

Today Mr. Moorman is host of this bed & breakfast complex. The former mayor even cooks and serves a "Covington" breakfast of eggs and homemade sausages (made with onions and sage).

Mr. Shinkle and Mr. Moorman: two men who became partners through the ages in preserving a lovely part of Kentucky history.

**BUILT IN 1854**

*The same year that Henry David Thoreau's classic book* Walden *was published.*

*This is one of seven guest rooms available at the inn. They are all furnished with antiques representing a range of styles and periods.*

*(Opposite) Even the stairway landings in this former town house are decorated with stately elegance.*

(Opposite) *An Oriental vase and a lacquered folding screen bring touches of the exotic East to a guest bedroom at the Amos Shinkle Townhouse.*

(Below) *This inn began as the home of Amos Shinkle, whose company built the famous Roebling Suspension Bridge between Kentucky and Ohio.*

(Right) *The parlor of the house welcomes guests with a fireplace, an antique music box, and a highly ornamented pump organ.*

*Amos Shinkle Townhouse*
**215 Garrard Street**
**Covington, KY 41011**
**Reservations: 606/431-2118**

**7 guest rooms in 2 buildings. Breakfast is included in the rates.**

❧

*The stately public rooms of the Hermitage are decorated with an eclectic blend of traditional, contemporary, and Oriental furnishings.*

# The Hermitage Hotel

## NASHVILLE, TENNESSEE

THE BEAUX-ARTS STYLE, a mixture of Italian Renaissance and Napoleonic French architectural details, flowered in the second half of the 19th century.

When a group of 250 Nashville partners wanted to build a luxury hotel in that city, they commissioned J. E. R. Carpenter to create the design. In a few months he returned with his concept, a Beaux-Arts, 10-story masterpiece using Italian Siena marble, Circassian walnut from Russia in a handcrafted dining room ceiling, skylights and glass panels fashioned by an Italian artisan, and transomed French doors.

The building would ultimately cost $1 million. When those French doors swung open for business, guests were invited into a hotel advertised as "fireproof, noise-proof, and dustproof, $2 and up." Everything was state of the art in the new hotel. Distilled hot and cold water circulated to all of the rooms, for drinking and for bathing. The

**STARTED IN 1908**

*The same year that Wilbur Wright set a new world's flight endurance record over Le Mans, France, of 1 hour, 31 minutes, 25 seconds.*

rooms were equipped with the new "talking machine"—the telephone—as well as electric fans and even a mechanical device that announced that mail was waiting. Each guest room also offered ample natural light, thanks to the U-shape of the building.

For more than 80 years the great and near great have been coming to this Tennessee landmark, the only commercial Beaux-Arts structure in the city. Many U.S. presidents have stayed here. So have celebrities such as Jack Dempsey, Bette Davis, Lily Pons, and Gene Autry. Al Capone used to show up too, although the hotel doesn't talk much about *him*.

But there is one bit of music history the Heritage proudly recounts. In 1949 a somewhat nervous young singer made her debut with a new song in the hotel's Grill Room. The tune was called "Near You," and the person who sang it was none other than Dinah Shore.

*The Hermitage is a 10-story hotel in the Beaux-Arts style constructed in 1908 at the then-staggering cost of $1 million.*

## The Hermitage Hotel

The Hermitage Hotel
231 Sixth Avenue North
Nashville, TN 37219
Reservations: 800/251-1908;
inside Tennessee, 800/342-1816

112 suites (bedroom, parlor, and private bath).

*This photo shows one of the hotel's 112 guest suites, each of which includes a bedroom, a parlor, and a bathroom.*

# Hale Springs Inn

## ROGERSVILLE, TENNESSEE

"JOHNSON! JOHNSON!" the cries rang out. From a small balcony perched on the side of the massive red brick inn, Andrew Johnson addressed the crowd. It was 1832, and the Tennessee tailor was just starting the political career that would ultimately make him the successor to the assassinated President Abraham Lincoln.

The inn was only seven years old then and was to witness many decades of history on its way to becoming the oldest operating inn in Tennessee. Originally known as McKinley's Tavern, the building became a haven for Union sympathizers during the Civil War. There probably weren't many block parties in those days. Advocates of the Confederacy met right across the street.

Late in the 19th century McKinley's Tavern became the Hale Springs Inn. Later still it was placed on the National Register of Historic Places.

As you walk through this inn today, note the many striking portraits of early-19th-century Rogersville residents. These were painted by Samuel Shaver, one of Tennessee's best-known early artists. The clothing and settings in his paintings provide a realistic sense of life in his time.

**BUILT IN 1824**
*The same year that John Quincy Adams was elected president by the House of Representatives (no candidate had received a majority in the electoral college).*

The three-story Federal-style building is notable for its symmetry and elegance. The original handmade bricks and mortar have remained in almost perfect condition over the years, perhaps due to a method of construction lost to later ages. The heart-of-pine floors are original, with the wood dating back to virgin forests in the area. Almost every item of furniture in the 10 guest rooms has its own story. The mantel in the Andrew Johnson Room, for example, was brought by wagon from Philadelphia in 1824. The Susan McKinley Room has an antique rope bed.

Perhaps it was those very ropes that creaked under the weight of the future U.S. president on that memorable night in the 1830s, when he made his satisfying speech from the nearby balcony.

*A charming gazebo provides a quiet, shady spot from which guests can survey the formal gardens of the Hale Springs Inn.*

(Following pages) *Pictured here is one of the 10 guest rooms at the Hale Springs Inn, all of which are furnished in the Empire style that was popular during the second quarter of the 19th century.*

(Below) *A Thonet-style bentwood rocker rests invitingly by a window in one of the Hale Springs' suites. Nearby a couple of logs are ready for use in the fireplace.*

*The Hale Springs' dining room bears traces of the hotel's origins as a rural tavern built in 1824.*

*Hale Springs Inn*
110 West Main Street
Rogersville, TN 37857
Reservations: 615/272-5171

9 guest rooms. A continental breakfast featuring homemade breads and cakes is included in the rate. Lunch and dinner are also served.

≈

(Right) *In 1832, future U.S. president Andrew Johnson delivered a political speech from the Hale Springs Hotel balcony, visible in this photo.*

(Below) *A impressive carved headboard dominates this guest room in the oldest continuously operating hotel in Tennessee.*

(Opposite, below right) *This night view of the garden reveals brick walkways laced with benches.*

*Before it became an inn, this graceful building in the Neoclassical Revival style had been the home of a prominent local physician and a school for girls.*

# Albemarle Inn

## ASHEVILLE, NORTH CAROLINA

IN JANUARY 1944, renowned Hungarian composer Béla Bartók, then in his fourth year away from his war-battered native land, was spending part of his winter in Asheville, North Carolina. He was staying at the Albemarle Inn.

Each morning he would sit at the window and listen to a chorus of birds greet the day. Perhaps, as some music historians later said, these avian concerts inspired Bartók's *Third Concerto for Piano*. He wrote the piece while he was a guest at the inn.

Located near the Sunset Mountains, the Albemarle Inn was originally constructed as a large home in the Neoclassical Revival style. Its owner had been Dr. Carl V. Reynolds, a physician and public health official who had gained national recognition for such pioneering achievements as the estab-

**STARTED IN 1907**

*The same year that Oklahoma became the 46th state in the Union.*

lishment of a school vaccination program for children and the requirement that bakers wrap all breads in paper.

After the property was sold in 1920, it became a school for girls. Then, in 1941, it was sold again and converted into the Albemarle Inn.

There are 16 rooms in the inn, most with high (11-foot) ceilings. The guest rooms are decorated with a mixture of Victorian and contemporary furnishings. Some rooms have fireplaces and claw-footed bathtubs.

Structural highlights of the building include massive oak doors and a carved oak staircase. The Albemarle Inn is now included in the National Register of Historic Places, a pleasant retreat for those who want to vacation in the high country.

Or perhaps write a concerto.

*Each of the inn's 12 guest rooms is simply but elegantly decorated, with private bathrooms housing old-style claw-footed bathtubs.*

The Albemarle's lobby and dining room have 11-foot-high ceilings, spacious showcases for flowers, and Victorian and contemporary furnishings.

Rooms like the one seen here have accommodated inumerable guests during the Albemarle's 50 years as an inn. Among them was Hungarian composer Béla Bartók who wrote his Third Concerto for Piano here in 1944.

*Albemarle Inn*
**86 Edgemont Road**
**Asheville, NC 28801**
**Reservations: 704/255-0027**

**12 guest rooms. A buffet breakfast is included in the rates.**

The inn's pool house can be seen at right in this photo. Guests who are so inclined can picnic on the lawn after taking a swim.

# Grove Park Inn and Country Club

## ASHEVILLE, NORTH CAROLINA

PHARMACEUTICAL TYCOON Edwin Wiley Grove of St. Louis (who made millions from his patent medicine formula for *Bromo-Quinine*) had an improbable dream. He wanted to build a sprawling resort in the Blue Ridge Mountains of North Carolina, one that would not just serve present-day tourists but endure "for ages to come."

But no architect or contractor of the day was able to satisfy his long-range vision. Finally he turned to his son-in-law, Fred Sealy. Mr. Sealy, having never designed or built anything before, agreed to create Grove's resort. This may have sounded like a plan for endless family squabbles.

But the results were a stunning surprise—a huge inn almost 500 feet long, made of steel, concrete, and boulders carved from the nearby Sunset Mountains. The "Great Hall" alone is a masterpiece, more than 120 feet long bracketed by two fireplaces

**BUILT IN 1913**

*The same year that Woodrow Wilson was inaugurated as the 28th president of the United States.*

capable of burning 12-foot-long logs. The Portrait Gallery features paintings of some of the inn's most illustrious past guests, including Will Rogers, Enrico Caruso, F. Scott Fitzgerald, Franklin D. Roosevelt, Dwight D. Eisenhower, and Mikhail Baryshnikov. (One literary note: when F. Scott Fitzgerald's wife Zelda was a patient at Asheville's Highland Hospital in 1936, Scott reserved the inn's suite 441–443 for the entire summer and wrote a number of his famous short stories there.)

The Grove Park Inn was later merged with a country club to create a total resort spanning more than 140 acres, offering everything from indoor/outdoor swimming and tennis to 40 meeting rooms and an 18-hole, par 71 golf course (played by Arnold Palmer, Jack Nicklaus, and Gary Player).

Mr. Grove seems to have attained his goal, a resort built for the ages.

*The Grove Park Inn straddles a 140-acre resort complex in the Blue Ridge Mountains, two miles from downtown Asheville.*

*Seen from above is the inn's airy Palm Court, a favorite gathering spot for guests.*

(Above)  *The inn's recreational facilities include nine tennis courts, one of which is in the background of this photo, as well as an 18-hole golf course and a complete sports center with Jacuzzis and saunas.*

(Right)  *This guest room—one of 510 at Grove Park—features some of the Mission Oak furnishings for which the inn is noted.*

*Grove Park Inn and Country Club*
**290 Macon Avenue**
**Asheville, NC 28804**
**Reservations: 704/252-2711**

510 guest rooms. The inn has many items of Mission Oak furnishings. All meals are available.

# The Ray House

## ASHEVILLE, NORTH CAROLINA

An EIGHT-YEAR-OLD THOMAS WOLFE may have walked by the new house under construction on Hillside Street as he went about the chores given him by his stonecutter father or his strait-laced mother (both to appear in fictionalized form in Thomas' first novel, *Look Homeward, Angel*).

The future writer would probably have been astounded to know that more than 80 years later the Ray House had become a bed & breakfast inn—with a bedroom named the "Thomas Wolfe Room."

There is also a room named for composer Béla Bartók, who stayed in Asheville in the 1940s. It shares a connecting bath with the "O. Henry Room." Another musician who frequently stayed at the Ray House during the 1920s was Lamar

**BUILT IN 1908**

*The same year that General Motors was incorporated in Hudson County, New Jersey.*

Stringfield, then conductor of the North Carolina Symphony. One of his compositions was used as the melody for the popular bluegrass tune "Cripple Creek."

The present owners, Will and Alice Curtis, continue Asheville's association with the arts in several ways. There is a library/music room with a grand piano. The guest rooms are furnished with antiques and arts and crafts gathered from around the world. And on the walls are a variety of prints and old posters.

Breakfast includes crusty herbal bread, lemon loaf (a house specialty), and Moravian sugar bread.

Thomas Wolfe was wrong in his oft-quoted, "You can't go home again." You can, if your destination is the Ray House.

*Seen here is the Stringfield Suite, named for Lamar Stringfield, a Pulitzer Prize–winning composer and frequent guest at the Ray House.*
(Opposite) *The Ray House sits in a grove of Blue and Norwegian spruces in Asheville, North Carolina.*

*The Ray House*

**83 Hillside Street**

**Asheville, NC 28801**

**Reservations: 704/252-0106**

4 guest rooms. A hearty continental breakfast is in-cluded in the rates.

❧

(Above, left)  *Author F. Scott Fitzgerald may have paused to admire this stained glass window when he visited the Ray House in 1938.*

(Above, right)  *Many of the inn's furnishings date back to the early part of the 20th century. The example seen here comes from the Béla Bartók Suite.*

(Below) *Visible at the end of the corridor pictured here is a doorway that gives entrance to the Béla Bartók Suite, named after the Hungarian composer who once stayed in Asheville.*

(Right) *The inn's homey dining room features such breakfast specialties as crusty herbal bread, lemon loaf, and Moravian sugar bread.*

# The Greystone Inn

## LAKE TOXAWAY, NORTH CAROLINA

THE HISTORY OF GREYSTONE INN could well be subtitled "The Case of the Disappearing Lake."

In the 1890s real estate magnate J. B. Hayes created the 3-mile-long Lake Toxaway high in the Blue Ridge Mountains of western North Carolina. It was to be the jewel of the beautiful Toxaway Inn that he soon built on the shore.

A guest of the inn, Lucy Camp Armstrong, was so fascinated by the setting that she commissioned the construction of a six-level summer mansion on the other side of the lake. This new home was shaped like a Swiss mountain cottage with balconies lined with flower boxes.

But Lucy only had a short time to enjoy the beautiful water view. In 1916, as she was rowing across the lake, she was frightened by a sudden swirling of the water around her. By the time she reached shore, the water level had dropped dramatically. Then the lake disappeared!

Headlines in the next day's newspaper told the story. Gorged by water from a recent hurricane, the lake had surged through an earthen dam

**BUILT IN 1915**

*the same year that Alexander Graham Bell made the first transcontinental telephone call, from New York to San Francisco.*

and flooded down the valley.

The now barren lakebed spelled the end for the Lake Toxaway Inn, but not for Mrs. Armstrong's dream house. She stayed on hoping for the best. "The best" didn't happen until 44 years later, when a group of entrepreneurs bought the dry lakebed and much of the surrounding land, built a new dam, and brought the lake back to life.

Today Mrs. Armstrong's home has become the Greystone Inn. Established in 1985, it soon earned the Four Diamond rating from the Automobile Association of America. The guest rooms are furnished with antiques and offer many contemporary luxuries, such as Jacuzzi baths. Separate family chalets are also available with full kitchens. Guests can use the facilities of the nearby Lake Toxaway Country Club, play tennis, swim, fish, and water-ski.

But guests out for a canoe ride may occasionally contemplate the uncertainties of this world as they dip their paddles into the lake that once disappeared.

*The Greystone Inn began as the Swiss Revival–style residence of Lucy Camp Armstrong, a visitor who fell in love with the Blue Ridge Mountain area of the Tar Heel State.*
(Opposite) *The porch of the Greystone Inn, with its white wicker furniture and area rug with a bold green floral pattern, provides the perfect setting for an afternoon tea.*

(Above)  *The inn's multi-windowed parlor provides splendid views of the surrounding woods and the largest private lake in North Carolina.*

(Right)  *This photo shows a quiet nook in the parlor, where checkers and conversation flourish amid antiques and period reproductions.*

(Opposite)  *A fieldstone fireplace dominates the dining room, where the excellent cuisine helped the Greystone become the only inn in North Carolina to win the American Automobile Association's Four Diamond Award. Another view of the brass deer at the edge of the fireplace can be seen in the lower left, and the mantel, with its antique clock and candles, is shown in the lower right.*

### The Greystone Inn
Greystone Lane
Lake Toxaway, NC 28747
Reservations: 800/824-5766 or 704/966-4700

19 guest rooms in the mansion and 12 lakefront rooms in the Hillmont, an adjacent separate structure. Two meals a day are included in the rates.

# The Fearrington House Country Inn

## PITTSBORO, NORTH CAROLINA

IN 1786 William Cole walked over the level forested land just south of what is now Chapel Hill—the home of the University of North Carolina—in order to plan a series of buildings that would house his family and serve his farm.

If he could see how these buildings are being used today, Mr. Cole would be astounded.

In 1974 Fitch Creations, Inc. purchased the land and buildings from the Fearrington family, descendants of the Coles, and began an extraordinary transformation of a farm into a modern country village. The brains and power behind Fitch Creations are R. B. Fitch and his wife, Jenny.

The farm granary became the Market, a country grocery store stocked with fresh-baked breads and local produce.

The milking barn was converted into a minimall with shops offering pottery, jewelry, and garden accessories.

**STARTED IN 1786**

*The same year that David Crockett, frontiersman and future hero of the Alamo, was born in Tennessee.*

The blacksmith shop became the village post office. The original Cole farmhouse was destroyed by fire in 1927, and replaced by the Fearrington farmhouse (now the Fearrington House Restaurant).

In 1987 a European-style inn was added to the country resort-and-home complex. It offers a Sun Room that opens onto a terrace and garden, and a Garden House Room with a fireplace. All of the rooms and suites have English pine antiques and original art. Other luxurious touches include marble vanities and heated towel racks.

Today guests can enjoy the countryside, shop in the village, and try some of Jenny's culinary creations, which include mushroom sausage tarts, corn soufflé with sweet golden peppers, and fresh coconut cake with rum and orange filling.

*This photo of one of the inn's nine suites, shot from the four-poster bed, offers a hint of the Fearrington's sumptuous accommodations.*

*(Opposite)  Oak trees and a black locust shade the Fearrington House Country Inn Restaurant and the inn's expansive lawn, the site of many weddings.*

(Above) *English pine antiques and colorful fabrics— seen here in Suite #1—lend an air of drama to all of the Fearrington House Country Inn's guest rooms.*

(Left) *Pastel colors and area lighting give the inn's parlor a light, airy feeling.*

*The Fearrington House Country Inn*
**Pittsboro, NC 27312**
**Reservations: 919/542-2121**

**14 guest rooms, clustered around a courtyard. All meals are available at 2 restaurants in the historic village.**

(Above)  *In the dining room, guests can sample such culinary creations as mushroom sausage tarts, corn soufflé with sweet golden peppers, and fresh coconut cake with rum and orange filling. Dining guru Craig Claiborne calls the Fearrington House Country Inn restaurant one of the best in the South.*

(Following pages)  *The inn complex, which includes a country store and a post office, is flanked by flowering trellises.*

# Arrowhead Inn

## DURHAM, NORTH CAROLINA

HAVE YOU EVER WANTED TO BE AN INNKEEPER? It's a dream that many people share, but for most folks it has proven as practical as Judy Garland and Mickey Rooney shouting "Let's put on a show in the barn!" in those old Hollywood musicals.

But Jerry and Barbara Ryan *did* become innkeepers.

It was a goal they had nourished for many years while Jerry published a McGraw-Hill technical magazine. In pursuit of their fantasy, the Ryans frequently visited bed & breakfasts throughout New England. They even attended an innkeeper's "trade school" held in, of course, an inn.

Finally their dream took on shape when they found a white two-story Colonial-style house in Durham, North Carolina. They wanted a place with plenty of bedrooms. This building had six—four in the main house and two in the carriage house.

The historical background

**BUILT IN 1776**

*The same year that the Continental Congress tried to stimulate shipbuilding in the new nation by authorizing payments of $37 a month and a half-pint of rum a day to skilled workers.*

of what became Arrowhead Inn was a bonus. It had originally been constructed as a plantation house on a large land grant between the Eno River and the Little River and was located right across from a "Great Path" that had been used for years by the Catawba and Waxhaw Indians as they carried trading goods between the Virginia lowlands and the mountains.

Each of the guest rooms is decorated to represent a different historic period, from Colonial through Victorian times. Most have a blue-and-green color scheme which serves as a backdrop for the antique furnishings.

The Brittain Room is particularly inspired, with a private terrace, a canopied bed, and a fireplace.

Jerry and Barbara enjoy mingling with their guests at breakfast and in the evening, probably answering one question repeatedly throughout the year.

"What's it like to run an inn?"

*Each of the Arrowhead's guest rooms is decorated to represent a different historic period, from Colonial times—like the room seen here—through the Victorian age.*
(Opposite) *This white brick-and-frame inn originally served as the plantation house for a large land grant located next to the most important Indian trading path in 17th-century America.*

# Arrowhead Inn

*A full country breakfast with homemade breads and muffins is served each morning in this dining room. The antiques and period memorabilia have been collected by the hosts over the years.*

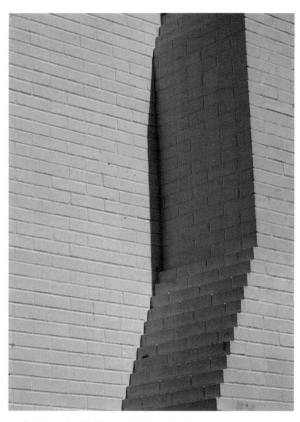

*This is a detail of one of the white brick chimneys that adorn the Arrowhead. The inn was built in the year that the 13 original colonies declared their independence from Great Britain.*

*Arrowhead Inn*
**106 Mason Road**
**Durham, NC 27712**
**Reservations: 919/477-8430**

**8 guest rooms. A full breakfast and afternoon tea are included in the rates.**

# The Lord Proprietors' Inn

## EDENTON, NORTH CAROLINA

EDENTON, with a population of a little more than 5,000 people, is crammed with more history than many communities 20 times its size. Founded in 1722, this picturesque town is the site of many preserved buildings dating back to the first half of the 18th century.

Three neighboring homes constructed in different eras starting in 1801 and ending early in the 20th century have now become the restored components of the Lord Proprietors' Inn. Owners Jane and Arch Edwards started the restoration of the oldest of the three, the White–Bond House, in 1982, followed by work on the Satterfield House and the Pack House. All of these buildings are certified as part of Edenton's historic district.

The three-home complex provides guests

**STARTED IN 1801**

*The same year that Thomas Jefferson and Aaron Burr tied for the presidency in the electoral college. Jefferson was then elected by a vote in the House of Representatives.*

with four common parlor areas, a separate dining room, and several porches, each surrounded by azalea bushes, dogwood, tulip, and crepe myrtle trees. Each of the guest rooms is furnished with antiques. The beds are unique, handmade by a local cabinetmaker.

Guests can enjoy a wide range of activities, from swimming in the owner's pool during the summer to winter weekends that feature suppers by candlelight.

One of the most popular diversions is simply walking through town and taking pictures of historic buildings: St. Paul's Church (1736); Chowan Country Courthouse (1767), the nation's oldest courthouse in continuous use; and the wonderful Cupola House, a unique example of Jacobean architecture (1775).

*Guests frequently gather on the inn's wrap-around front porch to enjoy the surrounding azalea bushes and dogwood, pecan, and tulip trees.*

*(Following pages) There are four common parlor areas in the Lord Proprietors' Inn, one of which is pictured here.*

(Opposite, above)  *From this front porch, guests can sit in wooden armchairs and survey the calm, peaceful world of Edenton, once the colonial capital of North Carolina.*

(Opposite, below left)  *Seen here is a room in the Tobacco Pack House, one of three restored residences that now make up the Lord Proprietors' Inn.*

(Opposite, below center)  *A colorful bouquet of flowers enlivens the bureau of one of the inn's 20 guest rooms.*

(Opposite, below right)  *A large 20th-century landscape painting adds a pleasant touch to the dining room, where guests gather each morning for cereal, fresh fruit, juice, and homemade breads with strawberry jam.*

*A conversation nook in one of the guest rooms is shown from the perspective of a four-poster bed. All of the beds in the guest rooms were made by a local craftsman.*

*In the sitting room of the Tobacco Pack House guests can find comfortable, stuffed armchairs and sofas for a bit of relaxation after a day of touring the Edenton Historic District.*

*The Lord Proprietors' Inn*
**300 North Broad Street**
**Edenton, NC 27932**
**Reservations: 919/482-3641**

**20 guest rooms in 3 different period homes. Breakfast is included in the rates.**

# Bay Street Inn

## BEAUFORT, SOUTH CAROLINA

As BARBRA STREISAND peered through the camera at the Bay Street Inn, gesturing emphatically with her hands, the film crew for the new movie she was directing, *The Prince of Tides*, completed preparations for the next scene.

To achieve the desired cinematic effect, two new palm trees had been transplanted in front of this riverside inn, and the picket fence and front of the Greek Revival building had been repainted.

Columbia Pictures had rented the inn for five weeks, and the town of Beaufort was seeing stars almost daily: not only Ms. Streisand, but Nick Nolte and Kate Nelligan as well.

But the inn has been in the limelight almost from the beginning. During the Revolutionary War, when it was only a one-floor dwelling, it had been occupied by the British. Later it was bombarded in the War of 1812. In 1852, it was completely rebuilt by a wealthy plantation family, only to serve as a Union officers' club after the Northern fleet had captured Beaufort during the Civil War.

**COMPLETED IN 1852**

*The same year that the first sewing machine was patented by Isaac Merrit Singer.*

Since the movie crew has departed, it's "quiet on the set" again, but the inn, located in Beaufort's Historic District, continues to offer guests a blend of history and charm. The owners have collected priceless antiques from all over America, including some acquired from the Winterthur Museum and Yale University collections.

The guest rooms are decorated with original art. The inn is surrounded by formal gardens with magnolias, crepe myrtle, and oaks.

When you go, you'll probably want to take many pictures of this historic beauty.

That's what Barbra did.

*Officers of the Union Army once may have read books in this library. The building was used as an officers' club after Beaufort fell to the Yankees during the Civil War.*

(Opposite) *The parlor, filled with valuable antiques, immediately calls to mind the plush plantation homes of the antebellum South.*

*Bay Street Inn*
601 Bay Street
Beaufort, SC 29902
Reservations:
803/524-7720

5 guest rooms. A Southern-style breakfast is served, including beignets and flap cakes.

(Below) *Looking at this quaint scene, it's hard to imagine the Bay Street Inn filled with the frenzy of Hollywood. But it was, when Barbra Streisand and a crew of actors and technicians filmed scenes from a new movie there.*

*Guarded by an ancient cannon, the Bay Street Inn, which was completed in 1852, stands in the heart of Beaufort's Historic District.*

*An Oriental rug, a fireplace, and a fine landscape painting add to the ambience of the inn's parlor.*

*Porches on two levels of the Two Meeting Street Inn overlook formal gardens with curved brick walkways and century-old water oak, Quonson cherry, and tea olive trees.*

# Two Meeting Street Inn

## CHARLESTON, SOUTH CAROLINA

THE TWO MEETING STREET INN is located in a house built on love and money.

In 1890, George W. Williams decided to celebrate his daughter's wedding in a spectacular fashion. He put a check for $75,000 on the newlyweds' bed, enough money to construct a large new home at Two Meeting Street. Then he sent the bride and groom on a two-year honeymoon to Europe while the house was being built.

All this largess may have sparked an interfamily rivalry for the young couple's affections, for while the wife's parents were building the house, the *groom's* parents bought Tiffany windows for the new place and had them installed by Louis Comfort Tiffany himself.

When the house was converted into a luxury bed & breakfast by David and Karen Spell, it took the name of its address—Two Meeting Street. It is flanked by gardens with

water oak, live oak, and dogwood trees and pink and white azalea bushes. Weather permitting (as it usually does in Charleston), a continental breakfast of fresh-baked blueberry and cranberry-orange muffins is served on a brick patio.

Each of the guest rooms is furnished with traditional Southern canopy beds and an eclectic mixture of antiques. A parlor is located on each floor, and there are several fireplaces, including one with a fabulous bas-relief blue-tiled mantel.

Guests over the years have included the woman who claimed to be Grand Duchess Anastasia of Russia (the only surviving daughter of Czar Nicholas II) and many, many honeymooners.

Mr. Williams certainly didn't realize what he started back in 1890. His present to his daughter and son-in-law has become a gift to newlyweds through the ages.

> **STARTED IN 1890**
>
> *The same year that George Francis Train traveled around the world in 67 days, 13 hours, and 3 minutes—a new record.*

*English antiques are used extensively in the decor of the parlor, seen here, and throughout the inn.*

(Above, left) *Dominating the staircase landing is a stained glass Tiffany window, said to have been installed by Louis Comfort Tiffany himself.*

(Above, right) *A statue of a young boy punctuates the inn's typically lush Charleston garden, where flowers are changed seasonally.*

(Left) *A detail of the finely-crafted glass window in the front door.*

*Two Meeting Street Inn*
**2 Meeting Street at the Battery**
**Charleston, SC 29401**
**Reservations: 803/723-7322**

9 bedrooms, all with private baths. A continental breakfast is included in the rates.

*Guest rooms at the Meeting Street Inn feature typical Southern furnishings, with canopy beds and period antiques. Wide bay windows offer a picturesque view of Charleston's historic harbor.*

# The Myrtles Plantation

## St. Francisville, Louisiana

A CHILD CRIES SOMEWHERE on the long porch stretching the length of the Myrtles Plantation.

But there is no child to be seen.

Later that night the sound of a woman's sobs is heard throughout the plantation. But the distraught person can't be found.

According to local tale-tellers the crying child and sobbing woman are two of the ghosts that have visited the Myrtles Plantation since it was built in 1796. Perhaps these otherworldly guests can be attributed to Gen. David Bradford, a former Revolutionary War officer, who insisted on building his new plantation house right on top of an ancient Indian burial ground.

Bad medicine, said the locals, and the ghost

**STARTED IN 1796**

*The first year gas illumination was used in the United States, in Philadelphia.*

stories have been coming ever since, prompting the *Wall Street Journal* to call Myrtles "America's most haunted house."

This dubious honor has been widely publicized by the plantation, which knows a quick way to capture the traveling public's attention. It has even attracted moviemakers who filmed *The Long Hot Summer* here with Don Johnson and Cybill Shepherd. Spirits or no, many guests come to stay in the antique-furnished guest rooms, to browse in the gardens of crepe myrtle trees draped with Spanish moss, and to attack the full plantation breakfasts of eggs, grits, sausages, biscuits, and coffee.

From March 1 through October 31, Myrtles Plantation gives ghost tours of the home for a fee. For ghosts the tours are free.

*Some of the antiques in the foyer of the Myrtles Plantation date back to the early part of the 19th century. The plaster friezework that extends around the upper perimeter of the walls is a good example of Neoclassical design.*

*Statuary enlivens the inn's garden, which is filled with crepe myrtle, live oak trees, and Spanish moss.*
*(Following pages)  Scarlett and Rhett would be right at home in the Myrtles' formal parlor, filled with many Rococo Revival pieces*
*from the second quarter of the 19th century.*

(Above, left) *The rear porch of the inn features an inviting rocking chair. Don't be too surprised, however, if the chair moves by itself.* The Wall Street Journal *calls Myrtles "America's most haunted house."*

(Above, right) *Breakfast is served plantation style (eggs, biscuits, grits) in this elegant setting.*

(Left) *This guest room—one of 12 at the inn— features such elegant touches as a circular convex girandole mirror, an easel painting, and a fainting bed.*

---

### The Myrtles Plantation

**P.O. Box 1100**

**St. Francisville, LA 70775**

**Reservations: 504/635-6277**

12 guest rooms. A plantation breakfast is included in the rates. Dinner is available by reservation.

# Nottoway Plantation

## WHITE CASTLE, LOUISIANA

*A*MID-19TH-CENTURY PORTRAIT of James Randolph shows a man with intense dark eyes, a long aquiline nose, and an aristocratic bearing.

The intensity of this Virginian transplanted at an early age to Louisiana quickly became apparent as he amassed a fortune in 7,436 acres of rich plantation land.

His aristocratic tastes came to life in the 64-room mansion he had built as the crown jewel of his estate. James watched over each detail of the construction, starting with the architectural drawings that specified an eclectic mix of Italianate and Greek Revival styles.

The front of the house and its circular wings were built with unusual square columns. Many of the mansion's innovations were extraordinarily modern for their time, including such novel ideas as hot and cold water plumbing, a gas-lighting system, and coal-burning fireplaces.

According to one legend, the house was saved from bombardment during the Civil War by a Union naval officer who refused to let his gunboats fire on the mansion. He had been a prewar guest there.

In 1985 an Australian purchased and restored Nottoway, now recognized as the largest extant antebellum residence in the South. Today Nottoway Plantation is an inn where guests enter through front doors 11 feet high, sit in front of the marble fireplaces that once warmed the Randolph family, and turn the same hand-painted Dresden doorknobs that once gave entry to ladies and gentlemen of the Confederacy. The 65-foot-long white ballroom is one of the mansion's highlights.

Many of the guests touring the inn are particularly impressed by two statistics. The Nottoway has 200 windows and 165 doors, an opening for each day of the year.

And the house was constructed at a cost of $3,800. Businessman Randolph certainly knew how to get the most for his money.

**COMPLETED IN 1859**

*The same year that abolitionist John Brown and his followers seized the Federal arsenal at Harpers Ferry, Virginia (now West Virginia).*

*An antique grandfather clock is the center of attention in this corridor of the Nottoway Plantation.*

*Nottoway Plantation*

P.O. Box 160

White Castle, LA 70788

Reservations: 504/545-2730

13 guest rooms furnished with Victorian and Empire reproduction pieces. Breakfast is included in the rates. Guided tours are available to the general public for a fee.

With 64 rooms, the Nottoway Plantation, featuring an eclectic mix of furnishings in the Italianate and Greek Revival styles, is the South's largest existing antebellum residence.

(Page 84)  This elegant white ballroom has been the site of many weddings over the centuries. Note the beautiful plaster friezework on the columns and the ceilings.

(Page 85)  The guest rooms at the Nottoway Plantation are decorated with original Victorian and Empire pieces, with some reproductions. Particularly impressive in this room is the elaborately carved bed with its imposing half canopy.

*The dining room at the Nottoway features such dinner specialties as Cajun Veal Panée and Smoked Quail.*

*A statue in the Nottoway's garden of moss-hung oaks.*

*A wrought iron fountain with cranes entwined bring the sound of trickling water to the inn's lush garden.*

*Sweet peas standing beside a red brick wall add a colorful touch to the inn's surroundings.*

# The Cornstalk Hotel

## NEW ORLEANS, LOUISIANA

ACCORDING TO ONE OFTEN-TOLD STORY, an early owner of the impressive mansion on Royal Street in the French Quarter married a young lady from Iowa. But shortly after she came to live in his New Orleans home, she began to pine for the wide farm vistas of her native state.

Her husband, wanting her to feel at home, surrounded the mansion with a unique fence; lacy iron work shaped like cornstalks "growing" from the ground.

The fence, which still exists, inspired the name of the mansion when it was turned into the Cornstalk Hotel.

The original owner of the mansion was Judge Francis Xavier Martin, the first chief justice of the Louisiana Supreme Court. Harriet Beecher Stowe was an early houseguest. According to yet another legend, she was so shocked by the sights of a nearby slave market that she was moved to write *Uncle Tom's Cabin.*

**BUILT IN 1816**

*The same year that Indiana became the 19th state in the Union.*

The rooms today have Victorian furniture, and the hotel is decorated with oil paintings and antiques. A front courtyard with a fountain and fish pond is framed by a brick wall covered with ivy.

Guests are greeted on arrival with complimentary peppermint schnapps. They can then wander among the many sights, sounds, and sumptuous restaurants of the French Quarter.

Many still stop and pose for pictures in front of that iron cornstalk fence, an affectionate touch of Iowa in the heart of the deep South.

*Did Elvis once look through this leaded glass window? It's possible. He, Henry Fonda, and Paul Newman have all been guests of the Cornstalk Hotel.*

*Although the residence that became the Cornstalk Hotel was built in 1816, the Queen Anne facade was not added until the end of the 19th century.*

This decorative wrought iron chair invites guests to simply sit and enjoy the pleasures of a sunny New Orleans afternoon. A fish pond and large cedar trees are highlights of the hotel's garden.

The Cornstalk Hotel

915 Royal Street
New Orleans, LA 70116
Reservations: 504/523-1515

14 guest rooms. A continental breakfast is included in the rates (juice, New Orleans–style chicory coffee, and blueberry muffins).

(Above)  A detail of the hotel's famous "cornstalk" fence, reportedly constructed by the original owner to soothe his wife who was homesick for her native Iowa.

(Below)  A vase filled with lush flowers, a decorative staircase, and a framed oil painting set the stage for guests as they head for their chambers.

# Soniat House

## NEW ORLEANS, LOUISIANA

By ONE OF THE CURIOUS PATHS of history, the Soniat House owes its existence to rebellious Native Americans in 18th-century Louisiana. Indeed, the mansion might never have been built had Chevalier Guy Sauhac du Fossat not been dispatched to America by the king of France. The king, it seems, had become alarmed by reports of Indian uprisings in his New World territory and sent the chevalier, a military engineer, to investigate.

Years later the chevalier's son Joseph, with the somewhat Americanized name of Soniat Dufossat, became an extremely wealthy Louisiana plantation owner. Befitting his station, he built a New Orleans town house for his large family, which included 13 children.

Today the Soniat House has become a small "boutique" hotel in the French Quarter. Many traces of the building's Creole origin are in evidence, along with newer architectural

**BUILT IN 1829**

*The same year that the first typewriter (a "typographer") was patented by William Austin Burt in Detroit.*

and design elements introduced by succeeding owners. The inner heart of the building is a lovely courtyard with a lily pond (where guests today breakfast on homemade buttermilk biscuits and New Orleans' famous *café au lait*). The thrifty Creole builders did not waste any space on interior stairwells. A winding staircase in a semiclosed rear area leads to the rooms. Later occupants added the lacy iron grillwork in front of the house, typical of many buildings in the French Quarter.

The current owners, Rodney and Frances Smith, purchased the property in 1981. They installed all new plumbing and electricity and began a room-by-room restoration using a variety of fabrics, colors, and antiques. One of the guest rooms (Reserve No. 24) so charmed a writer for *Travel & Leisure* that he dubbed it the "most romantic hotel room" in America.

*With its iron grillwork and colorful facade, the Soniat House is one of the most photographed inns in the New Orleans French Quarter.*

*This sitting room successfully utilizes a palette of pinks, greens, reds, and yellows,
which are linked together by the Matisse-like area rug and the naive painting above the mantel.*

*The Soniat's wide sweeping hallways bring together some of the hosts' English, French and plantation-style antiques, including the circular convex girandole mirror at right in this photo and an imposing chandelier.*

(Left)  *The second-floor balcony offers guests an enchanting view of Chartres Street in the French Quarter. Those with a taste for people-watching could not ask for a better spot.*

(Above)  *Exposed beams and a soaring ceiling give this suite's sitting room a wide-open feeling.*

(Opposite)  *The landscaped courtyard provides a plush setting for breakfast, where guests can dine on homemade buttermilk biscuits and New Orleans' famous café au lait.*

*Soniat House*

**1133 Chartres Street**

**New Orleans, LA 70116**

**Reservations: 800/544-8808 or 504/522-0570**

**24 guest rooms. A continental breakfast is available.**

# Terrell House

## NEW ORLEANS, LOUISIANA

THE LOWER GARDEN DISTRICT, built around the Coliseum Park, is one of the earliest residential areas in New Orleans. Many of the homes here were built during the first half of the 19th century, when every architect in the area seemed obsessed with the Greek Revival style.

The Terrell House, built for Richard Terrell in 1858, was no exception. It was constructed with many Classical Revival elements, around a large courtyard. Each of the families occupying this home added its own touches. Mr. Fred Nicaud, who collected antiques and gaslight fixtures, decided to convert the home to a guest house. Almost every room here is filled with items from the mid-19th century and illuminated by gas lamps or chandeliers.

**BUILT IN 1858**

*The same year that the first cable message was transmitted across the Atlantic, from Britain's Queen Victoria to President James Buchanan.*

In 1984 Terrell House officially opened as an inn. Guests may want to note the furniture in the rooms numbered 1 and 3. These pieces were made in the New Orleans workshop of Prudent Mallard, the craftsman who created furniture in the French style and helped furnish many of the area's early Greek Revival houses during the 1840s and 1850s. Marble mantels, gold leaf mirrors, and Mardi Gras carnival memorabilia carry the theme of Old New Orleans throughout the inn.

Guest rooms are also available in the original carriage house, all of which overlook the courtyard. The inn is located on Magazine Street, famous in the area for its antique shops and restaurants.

*As with almost every room in Terrell House, the second-floor bedchamber shown here is filled with items from the mid-19th century and illuminated by gas lamps.*

(Opposite)  *Terrell House, built in 1858, features a number of Classical Revival elements. The home was constructed around a large courtyard.*

## *Terrell House*

(Opposite)  *One of the highlights of the inn is its charming courtyard, a portion of which can be seen here.*

(Right)  *Terrell House features twin parlors, one of which is seen here. The mansion's original owner, Richard Terrell, would probably still feel very much at home in this room.*

(Below)  *Dominating the dining room is an elaborate Waterford crystal chandelier that the owner of the inn found in New York City.*

# The Burn

## NATCHEZ, MISSISSIPPI

SOME CONFLICTING IMAGES come to mind when you know the history of the Burn mansion.

Today the interior with a gaslight crystal chandelier, Belgian draperies, precious antiques, and old Paris china suggests a gracious and elegant past.

But now picture men on horseback riding past the Doric columns into the house, clumping past the beautiful spiral staircase.

That was the scene during the Civil War when some exuberant Federal cavalrymen claimed the building as a Union headquarters. As you look at this three-story Greek-style building, you can almost see a cigar-smoking General Grant pacing back and forth on the stairs on one of his visits here.

**BUILT IN 1832**

*The same year that Andrew Jackson was elected president of the United States, with 687,502 votes.*

After the war, the Burn reverted to private ownership. It remained a family dwelling until 1978, when then-owner Buzz Harper converted it to an inn.

Today the Burn is more reminiscent of the gracious antebellum period than the turbulent Civil War. Guest rooms include canopied beds, fireplaces, oil paintings, and flower arrangements. A full plantation breakfast is served in the dining room under an antique chandelier.

Then guests can stroll through four acres of gardens that are filled with camelias, azaleas, and flowering dogwoods.

They can also take a private tour of this historic home. Sans horses, of course.

*The garden at the Burn is enchanting in spring, when more than 125 azaleas, dogwoods, and other flowering plants and trees burst into bloom.*

(Opposite) *An imposing four-poster bed, a large girandole mirror, and an elaborate firescreen are among the antebellum furnishings in this guest room, one of 10 guest chambers in the inn.*

*A statue of a young bacchant is set against a black window shutter,
creating an interesting juxtaposition of forms, textures, and colors.*

(Above)  *The garden, where this settee now stands, gave comfort to Union soldiers during the Civil War, when the inn served as a Federal headquarters.*

(Above, right)  *This three-story mansion is an excellent example of the Greek Revival style that was so popular in the South during the early 19th century.*

(Below, right)  *The elegance of the South's antebellum period comes to life in the Burn's formal dining room, with its antique chandelier, brightly patterned rug, and floral centerpiece.*

*The Burn*

712 N. Union

Natchez, MS 39120

Reservations: 800/654-8859;

inside Mississippi, 601/442-1344

10 guest rooms. A plantation breakfast and a tour of the home is included in the rates.

# Linden

## NATCHEZ, MISSISSIPPI

EACH YEAR IN THE SPRING AND FALL the town of Natchez, Mississippi, organizes "pilgrimages" to the more than 30 antebellum homes in the area.

One of the prized stops is Linden on Melrose Avenue. This great mansion, listed as a National Historic Landmark, had a humble beginning—it started as a two-story cottage built on top of a gentle slope in 1792 by James Moore.

In 1818 Thomas B. Reed, the first U.S. senator from the brand new state of Mississippi, bought the house and soon began to enlarge it, buying more land and adding a 96-foot-long gallery to the front of the house and a one-story extension on each side.

Many years later the impressive entranceway caught the eye of the David O. Selznick organization, which filmed the doorway for a sequence in *Gone with the Wind.*

**BUILT IN 1792**

*The same year that the cornerstone for the U.S. Capitol was laid. The Capitol itself was not completed until 38 years later.*

The house was purchased by Mrs. Jane Gustine Conner in 1849. Her descendants have continued to live in Linden and now operate it as a bed & breakfast inn.

Linden is surrounded by century-old cedars and oaks in a park-like setting. The house has become famous for its collection of Federal furniture, with Sheraton and Hepplewhite pieces used throughout. The guest rooms have Chippendale, early Empire and plantation-made furnishings as well.

The west wing may be of special interest. It was built of brick because it was once the site of the house's kitchen and keeping rooms.

Linden has become an historic part of Natchez. Guests staying here may pause to consider just how old this house really is. It was begun when George Washington was president.

*An attractive silver coffee and tea service and two knife boxes rest on top of a sideboard in the dining room. Above them hangs a handsome framed print.*

*(Opposite) Looking at Linden today, it is hard to believe that the inn began as a two-story cottage. The front gallery and side extensions that were added in 1818 are clearly visible in this photo.*

*Linden*

*Linden*
1 Linden Place
Natchez, MS 39120
Reservations: 601/445-5472

7 guest rooms. A Southern breakfast
is included in the rates.

(Above, right) *The inn's seven guest rooms feature
Chippendale, early Empire, and plantation-made
furnishings, such as those in the bedrooms seen here.*

(Below) *A fan from India called a punkah provides a
comforting breeze in the inn's formal dining room.*

(Below, right) *Linden is surrounded by formal
gardens, which provide pastoral views for many of the
guest rooms.*

# The Steagall House

## OZARK, ALABAMA

ALABAMA CONGRESSMAN HENRY BASCOM STEAGALL was a man of considerable vision. He authored the Glass-Steagall Act, which created the Federal Deposit Insurance Corporation, and he was an ardent supporter of Franklin Delano Roosevelt. Indeed, FDR spent inaugural day in 1933 with Steagall, planning the bank holiday that allowed beleaguered financial institutions to close for a brief period of time so that they—and, by extension, their depositors' assets—could survive the impact of the Great Depression. Through these initiatives, Steagall became a significant figure in what historians later called the "Hundred Days," perhaps the high-water mark of Roosevelt's New Deal.

As befitting his station, Steagall acquired in 1932 a grand Greek Revival mansion in Ozark, Alabama. The home had originally been built for a district judge, G. A. Dowling,

**BUILT IN 1906**

*The same year that Theodore Roosevelt became the first American to win the Nobel Prize (he won the Nobel Peace Prize for his role in mediating an end to the Russo–Japanese War).*

and it later served as a hospital for a local physician.

In 1987, after years of neglect and a fire in 1986, the mansion was purchased by Rod and Lynn Marchant, who meticulously restored it and converted it to a 17-room inn.

Known for its Southern hospitality, the Steagall features antique furnishings in the guest rooms and public rooms. The cuisine, which Rod Marchant calls classic southern, features such delights as bobwhite quail with grape stuffing, acorn squash with cranberries and port, and sauteed veal chops with basil orange butter.

For those seeking outdoor recreation, there is horseback riding and skeet and trap shooting, and hunts for quail and pheasants can be arranged. There is also a croquet green and golfers are invited to use the facilities of a nearby country club.

*The Steagall House is a 17-room mansion, built in 1907 for Congressman Henry Bascom Steagall.*

**The Steagall House**

**416 East Broad Street**
**Ozark, AL 36360**
**Reservations: 205/774-0497**

6 guest rooms. A full Southern breakfast is included in the rates.

*The dining room provides an appropriate setting for classic Southern dishes, such as bobwhite quail with grape stuffing, acorn squash with cranberries and port, and sauteed veal chops with basil orange butter.*

*(Opposite) The entranceway, with its Oriental area rug and impressive chandelier, sets the stage for the rest of the mansion.*

*All of the beds in the Steagall House are handcarved from mahogony, walnut, and burl. The bed in this photo was constructed around 1845–1850.*

# York House

## MOUNTAIN CITY, GEORGIA

"*I* DO."

Many couples through the ages have repeated those two words in outdoor marriage ceremonies performed under a canopy of cathedral-like pines near the York House in Mountain City, Georgia.

That's appropriate because in the 19th century York House began with a wedding, that of "Papa Bill" and "Little Mama" York. They celebrated their marriage by building a two-story square-hewn log cabin on a 1,000-acre plantation in the Little Tennessee Valley of Georgia.

In 1896 the York's turned their house into an inn. It has operated continuously since that date, becoming one of the oldest mountain lodging places in northern Georgia.

**COMPLETED IN 1896**

*The same year that the first moving picture was shown on a public screen, at Koster and Bial's Music Hall in New York City.*

Over the years the inn has been maintained or restored with many of the York family's original touches, now turn-of-the-century antiques. The bathrooms are modern and plumbed with spring water.

Every morning guests can enjoy breakfast in bed, served on a silver tray. Afterward they can hike the nearby Black Rock Mountain State Park, raft some of the mountain lakes and rivers, or try fly-fishing for native trout in Sarah's and Warwoman creeks. In winter there's a choice of the southernmost ski resorts in the United States.

Small wonder that so many couples regularly return to this mountainous retreat, the setting of their original "I do's."

*Each of the York House's 13 guest rooms is decorated simply, with many of the furnishings dating back to the 1890s.*

(Above)  *The parlor provides a comfortable place for guests to gather and relax. Many of the windows have wonderful scenic views and anyone who is so inclined can always tickle the ivories.*

(Left)  *An Empire-style sofa and an antique mirror bring touches of the 19th century to the York House parlor.*

(Opposite)  *Guests are welcome to sit on first- or second-level porches and rock contentedly as they survey the lush north Georgia mountain scenery. Several hiking trails through the slopes begin near the inn.*

### York House
P.O. Box 126
Mountain City, GA 30562
Reservations: 800/231-YORK or 404/746-2068

13 guest rooms. Breakfast is included in the rates.

# Foley House Inn

## SAVANNAH, GEORGIA

THE MANY PARKS AND GREEN AREAS of Savannah, Georgia, are no accident of nature. In 1733 the city's founding father, Gen. James E. Oglethorpe, faced the wind on Yamacraw Bluff, clutching a sketch from the book *Villas of the Ancients* by Robert Castell, and laid out a town that kept nature close at hand. The general was centuries ahead of his time in "greening" a city.

Today a statue of Gen. Oglethorpe gazes across a sidewalk paved with oyster shells toward the Foley House Inn, a carriage house that in its own way—through touches such as its two courtyards— is reminiscent of an ancient villa.

A candelabra from the Tara set of the movie *Gone with the Wind* lights the staircase. Other dashes of antebellum romance abound, including crystal chandeliers, Oriental rugs, and fireplaces in many of the guest rooms. Several bathrooms are equipped with whirlpool tubs.

The inn was originally built as a town house by Honora Foley

**BUILT IN 1896**

*The same year that William McKinley triumphed in the race for the U.S. presidency over William Jennings Bryan.*

in 1896, an imaginative businesswoman who founded one of the country's early supermarkets in Savannah. The Foley House Inn was created from Honora's home and an adjoining town house. It is located almost in the center of the nation's largest historic landmark area (2.2 miles of historic preservation and historic sights beginning right outside the door).

Food is still a pleasant part of the inn experience, with a continental breakfast of bagels, fruit Danishes, croissants, and fresh fruit served in the guest rooms (on silver Norwegian trays) or in one of the garden courtyards.

Many of the rooms are decorated in the early-20th-century Edwardian style. Others have a rustic look. All of the guests enjoy such amenities as overnight shoe shines, cordials in the afternoon, and an outdoor hot tub.

Had he beheld this inn, General Oglethorpe might have said, "Well done!" as he paged through his well-thumbed *Villas of the Ancients*.

*A fountain with a deep blue basin and a nearby red brick wall add dashes of unexpected color to the Foley House garden of azaleas and tropical plants.*
*(Opposite) The inn was originally built as a town house by Honora Foley, an imaginative businesswoman who founded one of the country's early supermarkets.*

# *Foley House Inn*

*Foley House Inn*
**14 West Hull Street**
**Savannah, GA 31401**
**Reservations: 800/647-3708 or 912/232-6622**

**20 guest rooms. A continental breakfast is included in the rates.**

(Above)  *Horse-drawn carriages carry Savannah sightseers right by the front door of the Foley House Inn.*

(Left)  *Alongside the Foley House are sidewalks paved with oyster shells, which add a dash of rustic charm to the inn's character.*

(Right)  *The Foley House parlor is elaborately decorated, conveying the elegance of life in the late 19th century. Note in particular the elaborate wood carvings on the fireplace at left.*

# The Mulberry

## SAVANNAH, GEORGIA

TAKE A WALK through the Mulberry today and you would never guess its early history.

Open the paneled oak doors to a marble-floored reception area. Further on, the flooring in the lobby area becomes heart-of-pine wood reclaimed from old Savannah buildings.

Would you guess that this building began life as a livery stable?

In 1982, the Mulberry became an inn. At the time, it was owned by Days Inn, a hotel chain. Six years later, in 1988, it was purchased by the current owner, who undertook an extensive renovation of the building.

The walls are paneled with either golden or red oak. The public areas are filled with antiques—a Sheraton desk dating back to 1820, Empire game tables,

**BUILT IN 1860**

*The same year that the price of haircuts in Chicago was increased from 10 to 12 cents.*

French 24-karat gold lamps.

Would you guess that at the turn of the century this building was filled with steaming vats and bustling workers? That was during its days as a Coca-Cola bottling plant.

The transformation of the Mulberry to an inn is now complete. Guests are offered everything from afternoon tea to a rooftop Jacuzzi. Guest rooms are decorated with historic fabrics and furnished with Queen Anne, Hepplewhite, and Chippendale reproductions.

One of the many gracious features of this three-story building is the bricked courtyard, with gas lights, trees, and flowers.

The inn overlooks the riverside park, in the center of Historic Savannah.

*It is hard to imagine it today, but this beautiful building was once a livery stable and later a Coca-Cola bottling plant.*
(Opposite) *The inn's café overlooks a flowering courtyard and fountain.*

The Mulberry's elegant library invites guests to browse the shelves for a good book and to enjoy an afternoon of reading by the fireplace.

*Spectacular white Corinthian columns and a sleek chandelier add drama to the inn's foyer.*

*The Mulberry*

**601 East Bay Street**
**Savannah, GA 31401**
**Reservations: 800/554-5544**

**97 guest rooms and 24 one-bed-room suites.**

*In the courtyard, rows of elaborate wrought iron chairs set up for a wedding create a pattern that is almost hypnotic.*

# Hotel Place St. Michel

## CORAL GABLES, FLORIDA

GEORGE MERRICK may have been born the son of a conservative Pennsylvania minister, but he had the promotional soul of a Barnum or Ziegfeld. When he laid out the streets of his new Florida community, Coral Gables, he dubbed the canal-lined town the "new Venice." He even hired silver-tongued orator/politician William Jennings Bryan to lecture prospective buyers on the value of real estate in this sun-drenched mecca. And lest they get bored between sales pitches, he hired Paul Whiteman and the chorus from Earl Carroll's *Vanities* to entertain them.

Amid all of this jazz-age sound and fury, the construction of a neo-Mediterranean building for doctors and lawyers in downtown Coral Gables seemed only a whisper. A year after the office building was finished, it was converted into the small, intimate Hotel Seville—primarily to cater to the

**BUILT IN 1926**

*The same year that James Joseph "Gene" Tunney won the heavyweight boxing crown by beating Jack Dempsey on points.*

wealthy and famous who came to place their bets at the nearby Tropical Race Track.

In 1979 restaurateur Stuart Bornstein and his partner Alan Potamkin completely restored the building, renaming it Hotel Place St. Michel but keeping the Moorish arches, high ceiling, and the hand-set Spanish tiles in the lobby. Each of the guest rooms has been redecorated with English and French antiques and Oriental rugs.

The Restaurant St. Michel on the ground floor has won numerous awards with dining surprises such as Poulet Grille Key West (breast of chicken served with mango and papaya relish) and Crepe Oscar (stuffed with fresh asparagus, lobster, and chicken).

The famous Venetian swimming pool shaped from coral is a short walk from the hotel—sans Mr. Carroll's dancing girls, alas.

*The owners of the Hotel Place St. Michel call the furnishings in the guest rooms "Victorian eclectic."*
*(Opposite)  A continental cuisine is served in the hotel's ground-floor restaurant on Alcazar Avenue.*

*Reflected in a mirrored clothes closet with its elaborate marquetry is one of the 24 guest rooms in this small European-style hotel.*

*Hotel Place St. Michel*

**162 Alcazar Avenue**
**Coral Gables, FL 33134**
**Reservations: 305/444-1666**

27 rooms including 3 suites. A continental breakfast is included in the rates.

*Through the dramatic entranceway to Hotel Place St. Michel, pictured here, have passed such notables as Harrison Ford, Francis Ford Coppola, and Susan Sontag.*

# Casa de Solana

## ST. AUGUSTINE, FLORIDA

DON MANUEL SOLANA, a direct descendant of the first colonial child born in America, might be described as Florida's first real estate agent.

In 1763, under the terms of the Treaty of Paris, Spain ceded Florida to the British. But the Spanish residents of St. Augustine wanted compensation for their homes before they returned to the land of their birth. Don Manuel Solana stepped in to help sell their properties and settle the claims.

Even before he began this daunting task, Señor Solana had built a home for himself, a handsome colonial dwelling faced with scored stucco and supported by handhewn beams.

Today the Casa de Solana has become an equally handsome inn graced by the patina

**BUILT CIRCA 1763**

*The same year that Pontiac, the Ottowa Indian chief, laid siege to Fort Detroit.*

of more than two centuries. Guests can choose from four suites, some with fireplaces. Many of the windows offer great views of Matanzas Bay or of the flowering walled garden that surrounds the inn.

A full breakfast of Southern specialties such as grits, eggs, and fruit-nut bread is served in the dining room on a 10-foot-long mahogany table. Guests are invited to share a decanter of sherry. They are also invited to borrow bicycles for an easy, fuel-efficient way of touring the oldest city in America.

The fireplace in the dining room is an exact replica of one in the Oval Office of the White House.

Señor Solana would probably still feel right at home here.

*The Casa de Solana was built in 1763 as the private home of Don Manuel Solana, a direct descendant of the first colonial child born in America.*

(Above)  *A colorful floral arrangement and a ceramic tea service rest atop a piano in the Casa de Solana's formal dining room.*

(Above, right)  *Exposed ceiling beams and a three-tiered birdcage are among the charming touches in this guest-suite sitting room.*

*Casa de Solana*
**21 Aviles Street**
**St. Augustine, FL 32084**
**Reservations: 904/824-3555**

**4 suites. A full breakfast is included in the rates.**

*Couples seeking a romantic retreat would be hard-pressed to find a more conducive setting than this suite. It even has a sunken "marriage tub," which can be seen in the upper left in this photo.*

*Scrambled eggs, grits, and home-baked breads are among the featured attractions of the complimentary breakfast
served each morning in this dining room.*

## Acknowledgment

The producers of *Historic Inns of the South* gratefully acknowledge the assistance of the innkeepers whose fine lodging places are the subject of this book.